Contents

W9-AZZ-959

What are monster trucks?.................................4

Bigfoot monster trucks.................................6

Monster stars.................................8

Truck stunts and tricks.................................10

Car crushers.................................12

Monster racers.................................14

Road giants.................................16

Monster miners.................................18

NASA's giants.................................20

Activities.................................22

Glossary.................................23

Index.................................24

What are monster trucks?

Monster trucks are the world's biggest, fastest, and most powerful trucks.

Monster trucks with extra-large wheels thrill the crowds at truck shows, while other giant trucks move the biggest and heaviest loads.

tire

Mighty Machines

MORE MONSTER TRUCKS

Ian Graham

QEB Publishing

This edition published by Scholastic Inc.,
557 Broadway, New York, NY 10012
by arrangement with Quarto publishing.

Distributed by
Scholastic Canada Ltd., Markham, Ontario
Grolier International, Inc.,
Makati City, Philippines

Copyright © QEB Publishing 2013

First published in the United States by
QEB Publishing, Inc.
3 Wrigley, Suite A
Irvine, CA 92618

www.qed-publishing.co.uk

Written by Ian Graham

Designed by Phil and Traci Morash (Fineline Studios)
Editor Paul Manning

Picture Researcher Claudia Tate

A CIP record for this book is available from the Library
of Congress.

ISBN: 978-0-545-58530-9

Printed in Guangdong, China

10 9 8 7 6 5 4 3 2

Words in **bold** can be found in the glossary on page 23.

Picture credits
Key: t = top, b = bottom, FC = front cover

AFP/Getty Images Oliver Lang 16
Artemis Images Pikes Peak Hill Climb 10
Clive Featherby 9t
Corbis Duomo/Corbi 4, Richard T Nowitz 17, Transtock

When a huge load has to be moved by road, only a giant truck can do the job.

Monster trucks often have tires as tall as a normal-sized car!

Bigfoot
monster trucks

The world's first monster truck was Bigfoot 1. It was built in 1975 from an ordinary **pick-up truck**, but special wheels and parts were added to make it bigger and better.

The wheels of Bigfoot trucks are so huge that kids can easily stand inside them!

Bigfoot Fastrax is different from the other Bigfoots because it has tank tracks instead of wheels.

After Bigfoot 1, many more Bigfoot monster trucks were built.

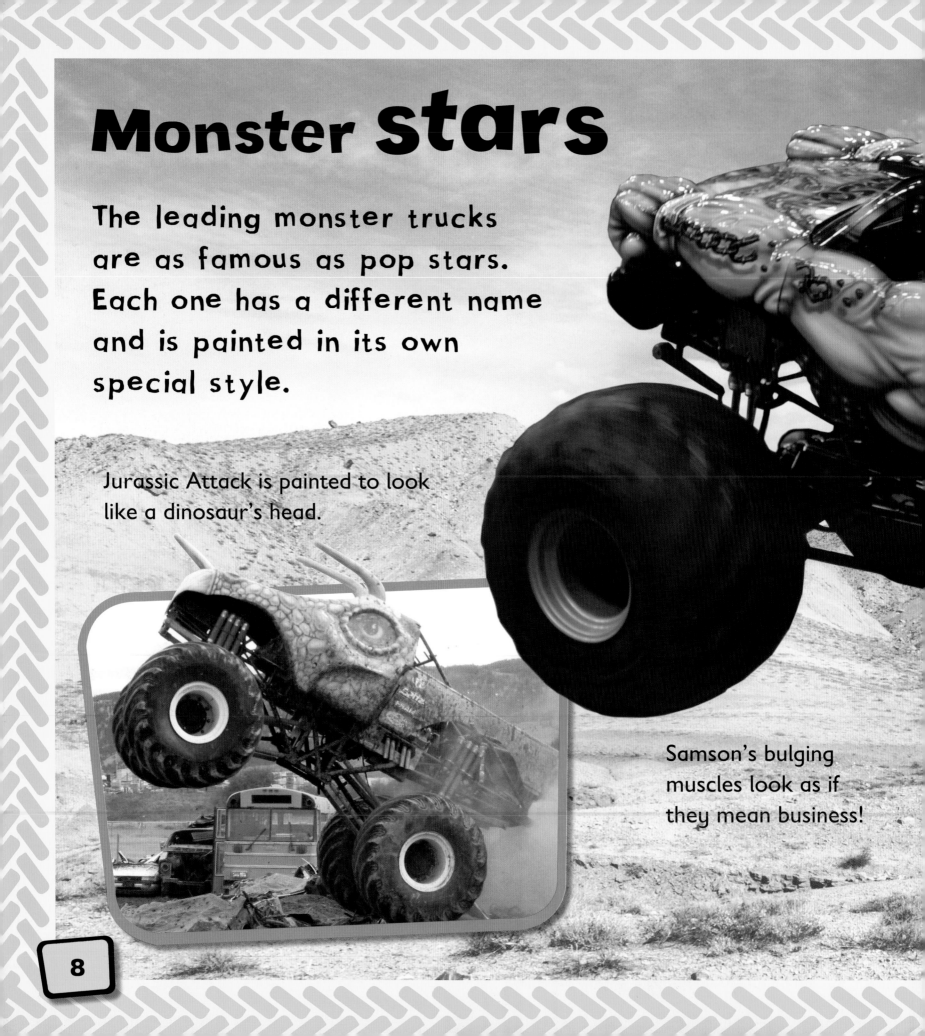

Monster **stars**

The leading monster trucks are as famous as pop stars. Each one has a different name and is painted in its own special style.

Jurassic Attack is painted to look like a dinosaur's head.

Samson's bulging muscles look as if they mean business!

Fans of the trucks cheer them on as they battle it out in competitions and races.

Truck stunts and tricks

In the **freestyle** part of a monster truck show, drivers make their trucks do amazing tricks and stunts.

The crowds love to see the trucks jump into the air, ride over ramps, do **wheelies**, and spin around on end!

The roof of a monster truck must be strong to protect the driver if the truck turns over.

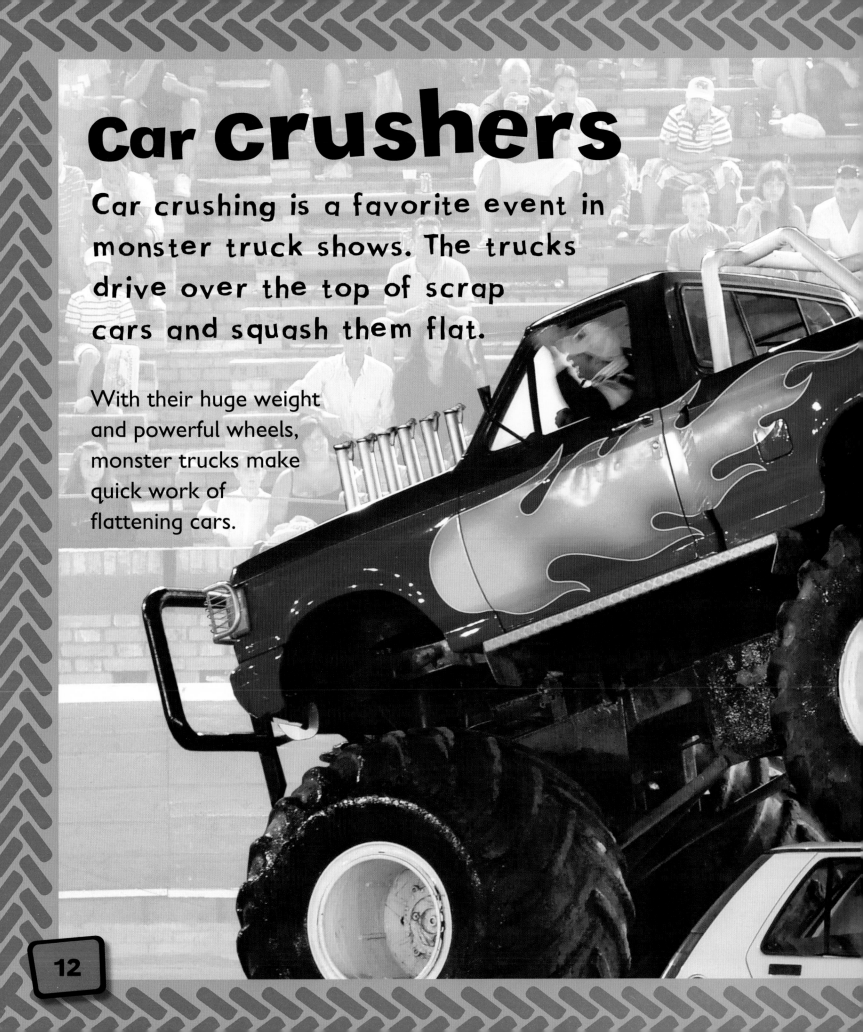

Car Crushers

Car crushing is a favorite event in monster truck shows. The trucks drive over the top of scrap cars and squash them flat.

With their huge weight and powerful wheels, monster trucks make quick work of flattening cars.

A monster truck jumps into the air during a freestyle competition.

How would YOU like a ride in this champion car crusher?

To make car crushing safe, car **batteries**, **fuel**, and glass must be removed first. Drivers must also wear fireproof suits and crash helmets.

Monster **racers**

Races between monster trucks are held in **stadiums**, on race tracks, and on closed roads. In a hill climb, the trucks race up a dirt track to the top of a hill.

This powerful racing truck is taking part in an off-road race.

Big crowds turn out
to watch their favorite
trucks compete in races
and other stadium events.

Not all racing trucks are giant-sized. Some are ordinary road trucks. Others are built especially for racing on **circuits.**

Road giants

While monster trucks and car crushers entertain the crowds, hardworking giant trucks **haul** some of the biggest, heaviest, and longest loads ever carried on wheels.

This huge trailer is carrying parts of an Airbus A380—the biggest aircraft ever built!

tractor

trailer

The part of the truck that does the pulling is called the tractor. Behind it, the trailer carries the load.

Imagine seeing a whole house coming toward you along the road!

OVERSIZE LOAD

Monster miners

The biggest trucks in the world are called dump trucks. Their job is to haul huge loads of rock dug from under the ground. The rock often contains valuable metals, such as copper.

The biggest dump trucks are so huge that the driver has to climb a set of steps to reach the **cab**.

cab

Giant dump trucks need even bigger machines to load them.

These trucks can never leave the **mines** where they work, because they are much too big to go on ordinary roads.

NASA's giants

The space agency **NASA** has two giant vehicles to transport its huge space shuttle craft to the **launch pad**. These two monsters are called **crawler-transporters.**

Each crawler-transporter runs on eight **tracks** powered by electric motors.

tracks

space shuttle

The first crawler-transporters were built in the 1960s. At that time they were the biggest tracked vehicles ever made.

Because of their size, crawler-transporters can only move at a snail's pace. This huge vehicle weighs 2,870 tons (2,915 tonnes) and carries around 5,000 gallons (18,927 l) of fuel.

Activities

- Which of these trucks is doing a wheelie?

- Make a drawing of your own monster truck with extra-big wheels. Think of a name for it, and then color it to suit its name.

- Look at these pictures. Which one is a dump truck?

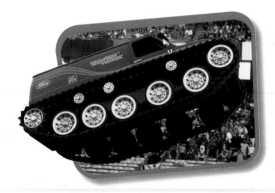  

- Can you remember what **NASA**'s giant crawler-transporters carry?

Glossary

Battery
The part of a car or truck that supplies electricity.

Cab
The part of a truck where the driver sits.

Circuit
A track built specially for racing.

Crawler-transporter
A vehicle that runs on tracks for moving very large or heavy loads.

Freestyle
Part of a monster truck show where drivers do tricks and stunts.

Fuel
Liquid burned in a truck's engine to provide power to turn the wheel.

Haul
To transport or carry by truck.

Launch pad
The platform from which a rocket takes off.

Mine
A place where coal and rocks are dug out of the ground.

Pick-up truck
A light truck with low sides.

Stadium
A sports ground with seats where people watch races and other events.

Tracks
Metal belts around a heavy vehicle's wheels to spread the weight.

Wheelies
When a truck stands up or drives along on just its back wheels.

Index

Bigfoot trucks 6–7

car crushers 12–13, 16
competitions 9, 10, 11
crawler-transporters
20–21, 22, 23

dirt tracks 14
dump trucks 18–19, 22

fireproof suits 13
freestyle
competitions
9, 10, 11, 23

jumping 10, 11
Jurassic Attack truck
8

launch pad 20, 23

NASA space agency
20, 21
pick-up truck 6, 23

racing 9, 14–15
road trucks 14, 16

Samson truck 8
space shuttle 20, 21
stunts 10–11
tracks 7, 20, 23
tractor 16, 17
tires 5, 6

wheelies 10, 22, 23
wheels 4, 6